THE 52-WEEK SEXUAL EMPOWERMENT JOURNAL

Mindi Miller

Welcome to

The 52-Week Sexual Empowerment Journal

This unique journal will give you 52 fun and effective weekly activities designed specifically to help expand and empower your sex life. Plus, the specially crafted follow up questions will help reinforce your positive progress and remind you of the growth you're experiencing.

The reason this journal doesn't start on a fixed date is because neither does life. We all move at our own pace and time. Your commitment to empowering your sex life might not begin on January 1st. We all evolve and grow at our own pace throughout the year. Every 52-Week Journal is designed to work with you on your own time.

Whenever you're ready, so is this journal.

You can follow the weekly order, repeat pages that specifically connect with you, or skip ahead to find new exercises and activities that speak to you where you are at any given time. It's all up to you! Positive sexual expression is about the freedom from life's many constraints. This journal's goal is to help inspire you to create a sexually positive state of mind whenever you want.

Many of the activities in this journal are designed to be done either on your own or with a partner. You might find yourself reaching for this journal every night without fail. You might want to take the occasional break. With the 52-Week Journal you always set your own rules.

So, open up this journal, and open up your mind. It's time to recalibrate your sex life with all of the desire and body positivity you want.

WEEK 1

Create a "Bang Box"
A dedicated container to keep all of your sex toys
and accessories in one spot.

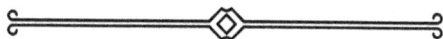

It could be a box, a drawer, or for the over-achievers
in the crowd, an entire closet. Whatever it is, just
make sure it's something you can easily reach when
needed. Assess if it needs a lock to keep curious
children or nosey roommates away. And make sure
to choose something attractive that speaks to your
design sensibilities. No one wants a dusty old Crocs
shoebox to be the first thing they see when reaching
for a sexytime toy.

Date_____

What container did you choose and what does it look like?

_____

_____

_____

_____

_____

_____

_____

Where are you keeping your Bang Box and did you have to modify it to keep anyone out?

_____

_____

_____

_____

_____

_____

_____

What is the first thing, or things, that you added to your Bang Box?

_____

_____

_____

_____

_____

_____

WEEK 2

Masturbate, to orgasm, in bed right before
falling asleep, every night this week.

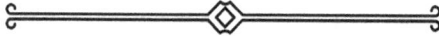

───────◇───────

Make sure you are ready to fall asleep immediately
afterwards. Plan ahead by having a towel or tissues
right next to you and the lights already turned off.
No checking email or getting up to wash your face -
make this the last thing you do before falling asleep.

Did you do this alone, or was someone else in the bed with you?

_____

_____

_____

_____

_____

_____

Did you sleep more soundly? And did you have any dreams you remember?

_____

_____

_____

_____

_____

Did you notice you were more sexually aroused the following days? Were you excited to masturbate again the next night?

_____

_____

_____

_____

_____

_____

WEEK 3

Create a secret sex code with a partner using regular, everyday comments like "I love s'mores" to actually mean something sexually related. Use the code words while you're socializing with others. They'll have no idea what you're secretly saying to each other.

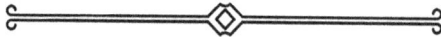

Make sure to keep it clean and not something you'd regularly comment on. Saying "The kids are driving me crazy" or "did you clean the bathroom?" can be confusing or crush the mood. Try using comments like "I love the smell of orchids!" or "Do you like glazed nuts?" to make your sexy intentions clear to only your partner.

Date_____

What are some of your secret sayings?

_____
_____
_____
_____
_____
_____
_____

Where and when have you used them?

_____
_____
_____
_____
_____
_____

What were the reactions and responses? Did anyone figure out it was code?

_____
_____
_____
_____
_____
_____
_____

WEEK 4

Invest in some accessories, props, or furniture that can make sex easier or more comfortable.

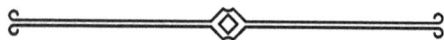

———◇———

Waterproof blankets, triangle shaped wedges and even everyday stepstools can help you get in, and comfortably stay in, all sorts of sexy positions.

Date_____

What items did you buy and what purpose do they serve?

_____

_____

_____

_____

_____

_____

_____

Did you find using these new items made sex easier or more comfortable?

_____

_____

_____

_____

_____

_____

Were there any items you already had around the house that are now used for sexual purposes?

_____

_____

_____

_____

_____

WEEK 5

One, two, three...some questions to get
in-depth about.

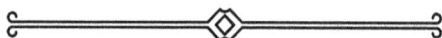

―――――◇―――――

Three questions to get to know each other better.
Answering intimate questions not only brings you
emotionally closer, but also gives a better insight
to what can be potentially pleasurable. Ask your
partner, or your friends, and share your stories with
them. The answers you get, even your own,
may surprise you!

Date_____

What is your definition of amazing sex?

_____
_____
_____
_____
_____
_____
_____

What is your best sexual skill?

_____
_____
_____
_____
_____
_____

What is the hottest sex dream you've ever had?

_____
_____
_____
_____
_____
_____
_____

WEEK 6

Lube, lube, lube.
And for the people in the back – LUBE!

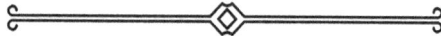

Lube isn't something just for old people and weirdoes, it's something damn near everyone should use to help make sex and masturbation more comfortable and pleasurable. Try different kinds of lubricants to see what you like best. With so many options to try - from the super slippery to the fully edible - shop online to read descriptions, making sure you purchase the right kind for the right situations. Reading reviews can help you choose the best ones for you.

Date_____

What kinds of lubes did you try?

_____

_____

_____

_____

_____

_____

What were your favorites? Are there any you'll likely not use again?

_____

_____

_____

_____

_____

_____

Did you notice any differences when using the various kinds of lubricants?

_____

_____

_____

_____

_____

WEEK 7

Create a Sex Location Bucket List.

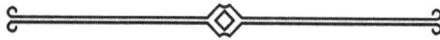

◇

List 3 – 5 places where you'd like to get naughty.
It's up to you how difficult you want to make this,
but I wouldn't suggest making them impossible
locations. Keep the ideas more broad in scope –
choosing sex in any locker room works better than
specifying your old high school locker room. If you
have a partner, they should also write a list so you
can compare what you each wrote.

Date_____

What are the locations on your list?

_____

_____

_____

_____

_____

_____

_____

Do you have a plan to make any of them come true sometime soon?

_____

_____

_____

_____

_____

_____

What were some locations that didn't make the final list?

_____

_____

_____

_____

_____

_____

WEEK 8

Video call your partner from the next room and
have them watch you masturbate until you're ready
to let them join you.

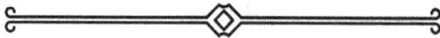

Make sure this is planned in advance so your
partner isn't busy working or not ready to focus on
your performance. Set the mood beforehand and let
them know they can't join in until you say so.
The anticipation they'll have waiting for your call
won't hold a candle to how they'll feel waiting for
the invitation to finally join in.

What was the response to just the idea, before you made it happen?

_____

_____

_____

_____

_____

How did it make you feel to make the call and put on the performance?

_____

_____

_____

_____

_____

What was your partner's response before joining you? And after joining you?

_____

_____

_____

_____

_____

_____

WEEK 9

Anyone can pay attention to the traditional sexytime body parts, so try using your lips and tongue to focus on areas that get less attention.

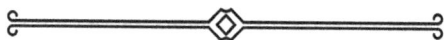

———◇———

Body parts such as fingers, toes, and armpits and can be incredibly sensitive and seldom get attention. Surprise your partner by giving some extra attention to the inside of their elbow and see what happens.

Date_____

What body parts did you focus on?

_____
_____
_____
_____
_____
_____
_____

What was your partner's response? And how did it make
you feel?

_____
_____
_____
_____
_____
_____
_____

Are there other body parts you want to focus on next? Do you
want your partner to try exploring your body next?

_____
_____
_____
_____
_____
_____

WEEK 10

One, two, three...some questions about
getting caught.

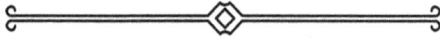

———————◇———————

Three questions to get to know each other better.
Answering intimate questions not only brings you
emotionally closer, but also gives a better insight
to what can be potentially pleasurable. Ask your
partner, or your friends, and share your stories with
them. The answers you get, even your own,
may surprise you!

Date_____

Have you ever been caught having sex?

_____
_____
_____
_____
_____
_____
_____

Have you ever been caught masturbating?

_____
_____
_____
_____
_____
_____

Have you ever been caught sexting or sending naked pics?

_____
_____
_____
_____
_____
_____
_____

WEEK 11

Invest in a remote controlled or app
controlled vibrator.
Give the controls to a partner or take matters into
your own hands.

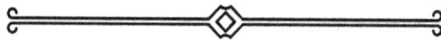

———◇———

Don't just save this for foreplay, try going about
your day, working around the house, or going out
somewhere while wearing the vibrator.

Date_____

Did you use the vibrator alone or have a partner control it?

_____

_____

_____

_____

_____

_____

_____

Did you go anywhere while using it?

_____

_____

_____

_____

_____

_____

Did it bring you to orgasm? If so, when and where did that happen?

_____

_____

_____

_____

_____

_____

_____

WEEK 12

Create a naughty scavenger hunt with clues full of
exciting sexual experiences.
If playing with friends make the clues full of
erotic questions.

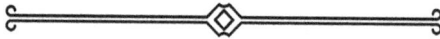

Clues with a partner can lead to items of sexy
clothing, fun toys or promises of specific sexual
favors. Clues with friends can lead to fun erotic
gifts or stories.

Date_____

Who did you play with and where did you play?

_____
_____
_____
_____
_____
_____

What were the clues?

_____
_____
_____
_____
_____
_____

What was the final prize or prizes? Did you end up taking advantage of a prize after playing?

_____
_____
_____
_____
_____
_____

WEEK 13

Invest in some sex toys specifically designed
for going solo.

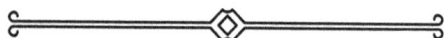

A suction style clitoral stimulator, a textured penis
sleeve or a wall-mounted dildo can take solo sex
to the next level. Sure, they can also be used in
the company of a partner – with some potentially
sizzling hot results – but you should always feel
good about investing in a little "me time."

Date_____

What toys did you purchase?

_____

_____

_____

_____

_____

_____

_____

Did you use them alone or with a partner?

_____

_____

_____

_____

_____

_____

Are there other toys you want to try?

_____

_____

_____

_____

_____

_____

_____

WEEK 14

Get a "happy ending" couples massage.
(Assuming they are legal in your location!)

———◇———

Erotic massages aren't just for pervs or sexless loners, they can be for anyone that wants someone else's hands to get them off. There are mixed feelings about whether getting a happy ending massage is a form of cheating, but it's not unfaithful if you're doing it together. Bonus points for getting all hot and bothered again by talking about the experience afterwards. Single folks can go alone, have a good friend join them in separate rooms or have a really good friend join in the same room. Not judging.

Date_____

What was the experience like for you?

_____

_____

_____

_____

_____

_____

_____

Did your partner have a similar experience as you did?

_____

_____

_____

_____

_____

_____

Was it exciting to talk about it later? Do you think you'll do this again?

_____

_____

_____

_____

_____

_____

_____

WEEK 15

One, two, three...some questions
about memories.

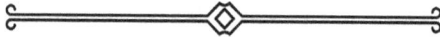

———————◇———————

Three questions to get to know each other better.
Answering intimate questions not only brings you
emotionally closer, but also gives a better insight
to what can be potentially pleasurable. Ask your
partner, or your friends, and share your stories with
them. The answers you get, even your own,
may surprise you!

Date_____

What is your first sexual memory?

_____
_____
_____
_____
_____
_____
_____

What is the best orgasm you've ever had?

_____
_____
_____
_____
_____
_____

What's the most embarrassing thing to ever happen to you during sex?

_____
_____
_____
_____
_____
_____

WEEK 16

Try light BDSM.

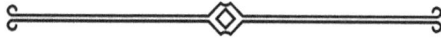

———◇———

Blindfolds, hands or feet tied up, a hand or tape over the mouth, light spanking, hair pulling, and being pinned down are all gentle versions of BDSM. Plus it doesn't always have to be the same person being dominated by the other, plenty of people like it both ways. Even if you're going solo, some of these can still be used to enjoy the experience.

Date_____

What were some of the things you tried?

_____

_____

_____

_____

_____

_____

Did you switch it up with a partner? Did you like it one way more than the other?

_____

_____

_____

_____

_____

_____

Do you think you might try less gentle versions of BDSM next?

_____

_____

_____

_____

_____

_____

WEEK 17

Have sex in front of a mirror, watching only what's happening in the mirror, like it's a movie.

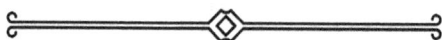

———◇———

Don't look back at your real body. If with a partner, don't look back at their real body. Don't even look around the room. Watch everything, as it happens, in just the mirror. The experience can be like watching your own sex tape, but live.

Did watching only the mirror make you feel more excited or awkward?

_____

_____

_____

_____

_____

_____

Did it feel as if you were watching someone else having sex?

_____

_____

_____

_____

_____

_____

Are there other positions you want to try in the mirror next?

_____

_____

_____

_____

_____

_____

WEEK 18

Create a signature move that you use before and during sex or masturbation.

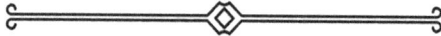

◇

Gently scratch your belly while masturbating. Nibble on a partner's ear while bringing them to climax. Choose a simple action that you can do every time things get hot and heavy so the brain eventually starts to associate that feeling with orgasm. Then, like Pavlov's bell, you can use your move during foreplay to quickly get in the mood.

What is your signature move and have you named it?

_____
_____
_____
_____
_____
_____
_____

What was the initial response to the new move?

_____
_____
_____
_____
_____
_____

How often did you use it during sex before trying it before sex?

_____
_____
_____
_____
_____
_____
_____

WEEK 19

Wear something sexy, lacy or fetish gear under your clothes and send sneak peek pics to your partner.

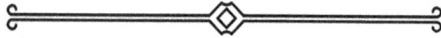

———◇———

Space out times throughout the day to send the pics. Only show little bits at a time. Keep the curious imagination going!

Date_____

What did you wear?

_____

_____

_____

_____

_____

_____

_____

How many different pics did you send throughout the day? And what kinds of pics?

_____

_____

_____

_____

_____

_____

_____

What was the response?

_____

_____

_____

_____

_____

_____

_____

WEEK 20

One, two, three...some questions about
sexy sounds.

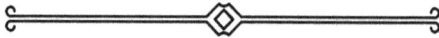

———◇———

Three questions to get to know each other better.
Answering intimate questions not only brings you
emotionally closer, but also gives a better insight
to what can be potentially pleasurable. Ask your
partner, or your friends, and share your stories with
them. The answers you get, even your own,
may surprise you!

Date_____

What is your favorite music to play during sexytime?

_____
_____
_____
_____
_____
_____
_____

What is something you hear that is guaranteed to get you horny every time?

_____
_____
_____
_____
_____
_____
_____

What sounds or words do you like to hear while having sex?

_____
_____
_____
_____
_____
_____
_____

WEEK 21

Create a Sex Toy Bucket List.

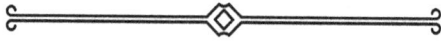

———◇———

List 3 – 5 toys you've never tried but think you want to. It's up to you how creative you want to make this – after all, the goal is to try something new.
If you have a partner, they should also write a list so you can compare what you each wrote.

Date_____

What are the sex toys on your list?

_____
_____
_____
_____
_____
_____
_____

Do you have a plan to acquire any of them sometime soon?

_____
_____
_____
_____
_____
_____

What were some toys that didn't make the final list?

_____
_____
_____
_____
_____
_____
_____

WEEK 22

Create a sex menu.

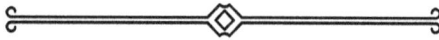

---◇---

Like a dinner menu with an appetizer, main course and dessert, but make it a multi-course sexual evening. Be specific – don't just say "foreplay" as the appetizer, but choose the exact activity you want to have happen during foreplay.

Date_____

What were the items listed on your menu?

_____
_____
_____
_____
_____
_____
_____

Did you make it all the way through dessert?

_____
_____
_____
_____
_____
_____

Do you now have more menus in mind?

_____
_____
_____
_____
_____
_____
_____

WEEK 23

Plan for sexytime in a hot bath or long shower with scented candles and sexy music.

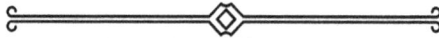

———◇———

Stress causes the muscles of your body to contract and tighten, so taking a hot bath can relax you physically and mentally. Use lots of lather in the shower to make cleaning your body feel extra special. Plan ahead for creative foreplay by bringing props like a wall mount foot stand or waterproof toys if you want to start the fun time in the bath.

Did the hot water make you feel more physically relaxed, sexually excited, or both?

_____

_____

_____

_____

_____

_____

What toys or accessories did you bring in with you?

_____

_____

_____

_____

_____

Will you make this a semi-regular thing from now on?

_____

_____

_____

_____

_____

WEEK 24

Naked dance party!

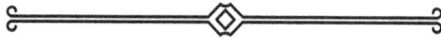

———◇———

Turn on the music and take off your clothes! Not only will dancing improve your mood, but it will also fire up your endorphins that boost pleasure and feelings of euphoria. And the best part is you're already naked, so taking advantage of all those endorphins will be even easier.

Date_____

What was your dance party playlist?

_____
_____
_____
_____
_____
_____
_____

Were you alone or dancing with a partner? Will you do it again?

_____
_____
_____
_____
_____
_____

How did it make you feel? Did you have fun? Did you feel fearless?

_____
_____
_____
_____
_____

WEEK 25

One, two, three...some questions
about watching.

———◇———

Three questions to get to know each other better.
Answering intimate questions not only brings you
emotionally closer, but also gives a better insight
to what can be potentially pleasurable. Ask your
partner, or your friends, and share your stories with
them. The answers you get, even your own,
may surprise you!

Would you prefer to have someone watch you having sex or watch them having sex?

_____

_____

_____

_____

_____

_____

_____

Is there a movie or show that always gets you sexually excited?

_____

_____

_____

_____

_____

_____

_____

What is a sex act you'd like to watch your partner perform on themself?

_____

_____

_____

_____

_____

_____

WEEK 26

Body Mapping!
Skin is the largest organ of the body; you
should get to know it better.

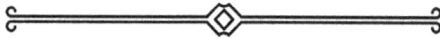

———◇———

From gently scratching your armpits to lightly
smacking your inner thighs, discovering new
sensual places on your body and the preferred ways
to touch them opens up an expanded world of
pleasure. Start at one end of your body and work
your way to the other. Or make this a date night
activity to get to know your partner's pleasure
zones even better.

What areas on your body were surprisingly sensual?

_____
_____
_____
_____
_____
_____
_____

Were there areas on your body that you didn't like to have touched?

_____
_____
_____
_____
_____
_____

Did you do this on your own or with a partner?

_____
_____
_____
_____
_____
_____

WEEK 27

Try mutual masturbation this week.
Get to know what your partner likes while letting
them know what also works for you.

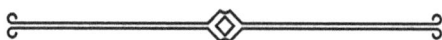

◇

Pick a comfortable position, anywhere from laying
side-by-side to sitting up and facing each other,
where you can both feel comfortable. Agree to make
sure you both get to reach orgasm. And remember,
this doesn't have to lead to penetrative sex, mutual
masturbation can easily be the main course.

Did you have a favorite position that worked for both of you? Did it start off awkward or exciting?

_____

_____

_____

_____

_____

_____

_____

Was it all by hand or did you bring some toys into the equation? And did it lead to penetrative sex?

_____

_____

_____

_____

_____

_____

_____

Did one of you orgasm before the other one?

_____

_____

_____

_____

_____

_____

WEEK 28

Role play!

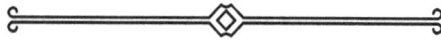

Dress up in an outfit or costume you've always wanted to wear, or ask your partner what costumes they think are super hot. It might be as easy as sexy teacher and naughty student or a *Fight Club* style naked Brad Pitt wearing one rubber glove. That's just the beginning of how creative you can get.

Date_____

What ideas and outfits came up?

_____

_____

_____

_____

_____

_____

_____

What was the first role-play adventure you tried?

_____

_____

_____

_____

_____

_____

How did it go? Was it exciting or awkward?

_____

_____

_____

_____

_____

_____

_____

WEEK 29

Binge watch some sex-positive TV shows.

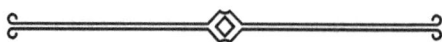

———————◇———————

There is no shortage of mainstream TV shows
portraying healthy views on modern day sex lives.
Watching these shows can give you a positive
outlook on empowered sexual behavior,
and no worries about someone seeing what
you've been streaming.

Date_____

What shows did you watch?

_____
_____
_____
_____
_____
_____
_____

Did you change or expand your feelings about your sexual desires?

_____
_____
_____
_____
_____
_____

Will you watch these shows with a partner or friends so you discuss them?

_____
_____
_____
_____
_____

WEEK 30

One, two, three...some questions
about fantasies.

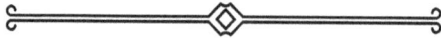

———◇———

Three questions to get to know each other better.
Answering intimate questions not only brings you
emotionally closer, but also gives a better insight
to what can be potentially pleasurable. Ask your
partner, or your friends, and share your stories with
them. The answers you get, even your own,
may surprise you!

Have you ever thought about swapping partners and did it excite you or make you uncomfortable?

_____

_____

_____

_____

_____

What is a sex act you've always wanted to try but never had the chance to?

_____

_____

_____

_____

_____

If you could have sex with one famous person who would it be?

_____

_____

_____

_____

_____

WEEK 31

Search for images of various sex positions and, because the term "doggy style" is boring, come up with your own new names for the positions.

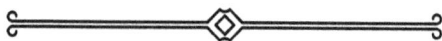

———◇———

From "The lazy frog" to "Chairman of the board" and "Beats a stick in the eye," try to have the name reflect the position. Get creative or get silly, either way, make it your own. Then later on, ask for the positions you want to try using the new names you came up with. See if your partner can guess what the positions are.

What positions did you rename?

_____

_____

_____

_____

_____

_____

_____

Did you use the new names to ask for sex? Did your partner figure them out?

_____

_____

_____

_____

_____

_____

Did you share the new names with any friends? Did they have other suggestions?

_____

_____

_____

_____

_____

WEEK 32

Schedule sexual activities.

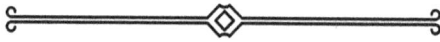

———◇———

Pick a certain day, or days, of the week for sex to be a priority. Really look forward to that day, planning what toys you'll use or outfit you'll wear. Making your sexual health a priority will not only get you physically hot, it's also good for your mental health.

Date_____

What day(s) of the week did you choose for your sexual activity?

_____

_____

_____

_____

_____

_____

Did you stick to the sex calendar? Was it difficult to stick with it?

_____

_____

_____

_____

_____

Did you notice an attitude change about sex by having it scheduled?

_____

_____

_____

_____

_____

_____

_____

WEEK 33

Create a Sex Position List.

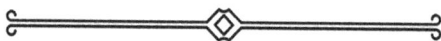

———◇———

List 3 – 5 positions you've never tried but think you want to. It's up to you how challenging you want to make this, but I wouldn't suggest making them impossible – after all, the goal is to succeed and try something new. If you have a partner, they should also write a list so you can compare what you each wrote.

Date_____

What are the positions on your list?

_____

_____

_____

_____

_____

_____

_____

Do you have a plan to try any of them sometime soon?

_____

_____

_____

_____

_____

_____

What were some positions that didn't make the final list?

_____

_____

_____

_____

_____

_____

_____

WEEK 34

Read an erotic book out loud.

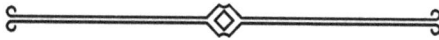

―――――◇―――――

From voyeurism, to feminist porn to sex with mermen, there's a modern erotic book out there for everyone. Don't want to be caught buying so-called trashy novels? Dive into *The Outlander* series by Diana Gabaldon for some mainstream wet dreams.

Date_____

What book did you choose and how did you choose it?

_____

_____

_____

_____

_____

_____

Did you read it every night this week or space out the fun?

_____

_____

_____

_____

_____

_____

Did you have any erotic dreams after reading it?

_____

_____

_____

_____

_____

_____

71

WEEK 35

One, two, three...some questions
about locations.

———◇———

Three questions to get to know each other better.
Answering intimate questions not only brings you
emotionally closer, but also gives a better insight
to what can be potentially pleasurable. Ask your
partner, or your friends, and share your stories with
them. The answers you get, even your own,
may surprise you!

Date_____

Where is the craziest place you ever hooked up with someone?

_____
_____
_____
_____
_____
_____

If you could have sex any location in the world where would that be?

_____
_____
_____
_____
_____
_____

Is there an odd room in the house where you would you like to have sex?

_____
_____
_____
_____
_____

73

WEEK 36

Discuss any interest in anal play.
Not sure you know yet?
Try it solo first.

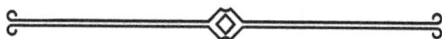

Anal sex can be a big fail without a lot of prep work.
It's not quick and easy like what you see in porn.
The actors prep for the scene well in advance and
add lots of lube before the camera starts rolling.
Did I mention Lube? Seriously, LUBE.

Date_____

How did the conversation go?

_____
_____
_____
_____
_____
_____
_____

What prep work did you do?

_____
_____
_____
_____
_____
_____

Did you enjoy the experience? Want to try it again?

_____
_____
_____
_____
_____
_____
_____

WEEK 37

Watch some erotic movies.
Whether watching alone or watching with a partner,
it's a great way to get the night started.

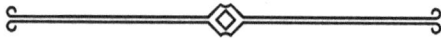

◇

For some, porn can be too unrealistic or a total
turnoff, but don't let that stop you. Look for adult
content that suits your taste - trust me, it's out
there! From Christian erotica to exotic kinks and
female friendly stories, there's a genre of adult
content for almost everyone.

Date_____

What kind of genre(s) did you find to turn you on?

_____
_____
_____
_____
_____
_____
_____

Were you surprised by some of the things that got you excited?

_____
_____
_____
_____
_____
_____

Was the sex hotter or more exciting after watching the movies?

_____
_____
_____
_____
_____
_____
_____

WEEK 38

Sign up for a sexy subscription box.

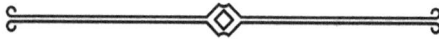

———◇———

It could be filled with lingerie, toys, accessories or food and wine - look online for a version that suits you. Then just wait for the sexy scheduled surprises you may have never found for yourself.

What kind of box did you sign up for and how often does it come?

_____

_____

_____

_____

_____

_____

What have been your favorite items you've received so far?

_____

_____

_____

_____

_____

_____

Has this inspired you to sign up for any other subscription boxes?

_____

_____

_____

_____

_____

WEEK 39

Experiment with CBD infused products.

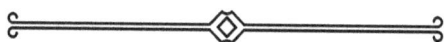

CBD can't get you high, but it can reduce anxiety, enable you to relax, decrease pain, and enhance physical pleasure. Sounds like a perfect fit for sex! From infused lubes, genitalia safe oils and medicated suppositories. When used inside the vagina or anus, they not only help lubricate the area, but the targeted effects can make a pleasurable difference.

Date_____

What CBD products did you try?

_____

_____

_____

_____

_____

_____

_____

What was your experience using them?

_____

_____

_____

_____

_____

_____

Do you think you'll try other infused products? Which ones?

_____

_____

_____

_____

_____

_____

_____

WEEK 40

One, two, three...some questions
about positions.

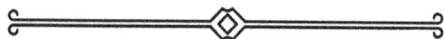

―――――◇―――――

Three questions to get to know each other better.
Answering intimate questions not only brings you
emotionally closer, but also gives a better insight
to what can be potentially pleasurable. Ask your
partner, or your friends, and share your stories with
them. The answers you get, even your own,
may surprise you!

Date_____

What is your favorite position to be in, or have your partner in, during foreplay?

_____

_____

_____

_____

_____

Do you prefer to be in control or be dominated during sex? Or both?

_____

_____

_____

_____

_____

Is there a sexual position you've always wanted to try but never had the chance?

_____

_____

_____

_____

_____

WEEK 41

Plan a naughty game night with friends
or a partner.

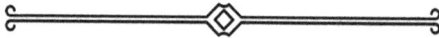

———◇———

Q&A card games, Spicy Dice, Honeymoon in a Box,
Bondage Seductions, Bedroom Rockstar, and Spice
it Up to name a few. The best part - playing sexy
games with friends might give you some sexytime
ideas you hadn't thought about before.

Date_____

Who came to play at your game night?

_____

_____

_____

_____

_____

_____

_____

What games did you play?

_____

_____

_____

_____

_____

_____

Were you surprised or excited by anything you learned?

_____

_____

_____

_____

_____

_____

_____

WEEK 42

Sign up for a sex class.

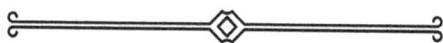

———◇———

Adult toy stores often hold classes on various topics, but you can also find them online. You'd be surprised at how much more you can learn about things that you thought you already knew about. Classes where people can ask live questions are especially fun.

Date_____

What was the topic of the class you took? Where was the class held?

_____

_____

_____

_____

_____

_____

Did you learn anything that surprised you?

_____

_____

_____

_____

_____

_____

Are there other classes you'd now be interested in taking?

_____

_____

_____

_____

_____

_____

WEEK 43

Purchase a sex swing.

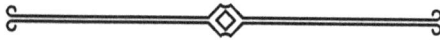

———◇———

There are several different styles and ways to hang them, so starting with an inexpensive, over the door version can help you decide if you enjoy it enough to upgrade to something fancier. Add a suction cup dildo to the wall or door for hands-free solo pleasure!

What kind of sex swing did you buy? How did you feel using it?

_____

_____

_____

_____

_____

_____

_____

Did you use it solo or with a partner? Did you use any toys while on the swing?

_____

_____

_____

_____

_____

_____

Do you think you'll upgrade your swing? If so, what kind?

_____

_____

_____

_____

_____

WEEK 44

Learn to find, and use, sexy acupressure
points on your body.

◇

Whether alone or with someone else, engaging
pressure points to increase libido, stamina, or
testosterone can add a new level of excitement
to your sex life.

Date_____

What was your favorite pressure point to use?

_____

_____

_____

_____

_____

_____

_____

Did the acupressure make you feel relaxed or stimulated?

_____

_____

_____

_____

_____

_____

_____

Have you learned how you use any other pressure points?

_____

_____

_____

_____

_____

_____

_____

WEEK 45

One, two, three...some questions
about favorites.

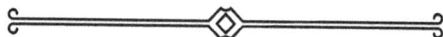

———◇———

Three questions to get to know each other better.
Answering intimate questions not only brings you
emotionally closer, but also gives a better insight
to what can be potentially pleasurable. Ask your
partner, or your friends, and share your stories with
them. The answers you get, even your own,
may surprise you!

Date_____

What is your favorite part of the body?

_____
_____
_____
_____
_____
_____
_____

What is your favorite time of day to have sex?

_____
_____
_____
_____
_____
_____

What is your favorite thing to think about when masturbating or having sex?

_____
_____
_____
_____
_____
_____

WEEK 46

Create a Sex Scenario Bucket List.

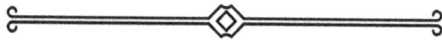

───────◇───────

List 3 – 5 story lines you'd like to enact while getting naughty. It's up to you how creative you want to make this, but I wouldn't suggest making them impossible to complete. Keep the ideas more broad in scope too – choosing a sexy pirate theme works better than specifying sex on an actual pirate ship. If you have a partner, they should also write a list so you can compare what you each wrote.

Date_____

What are the scenarios on your list?

_____

_____

_____

_____

_____

_____

Do you have a plan to make any of them come true sometime soon?

_____

_____

_____

_____

_____

_____

What were some scenarios that didn't make the final list?

_____

_____

_____

_____

_____

_____

WEEK 47

Read sexual self-help articles with a partner or friends.

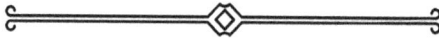

───────◇───────

Use the guise of discussing science-based information to open up the conversation about sexual ideas or requests. People are more likely to be honest about sex when you start the conversation with science and facts. Plus you'll probably learn something valuable too!

Date_____

What scientific articles did you discuss? Did you learn anything new?

_____

_____

_____

_____

_____

Who did you have the conversations with? What did you learn from them?

_____

_____

_____

_____

_____

Did this allow you to bring up other sexual ideas or requests you have?

_____

_____

_____

_____

_____

WEEK 48

Sit in a coffee house and make up sexy stories about the people there.

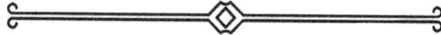

◇

Pick people that you find interesting or attractive and give them dirty backstories. Keep those stories in mind to fantasize about the next time you're getting busy in bed.

Where did you go? How many people did you make up stories about?

_____

_____

_____

_____

_____

_____

_____

Did you fantasize about any of them later?

_____

_____

_____

_____

_____

Have you seen any of them again? Did that make you feel excited or embarrassed?

_____

_____

_____

_____

_____

WEEK 49

Masturbate first thing in the morning, before getting out of bed, every day this week.

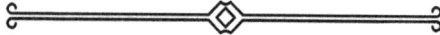

———◇———

Science has shown that orgasms can release dopamine, endorphins and endorphins – all called "happiness hormones" – associated with aiding relaxation and reducing stress. What a great way to start the day!

Did you do this alone, or was someone else in the bed with you?

_____

_____

_____

_____

_____

_____

Did you feel more energized, focused or relaxed during the day?

_____

_____

_____

_____

_____

Did you notice you were more sexually aroused during the day? And were you looking forward to masturbating again the next morning?

_____

_____

_____

_____

_____

WEEK 50

One, two, three...some questions
about your phone.

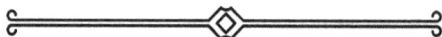

———————◇———————

Three questions to get to know each other better.
Answering intimate questions not only brings you
emotionally closer, but also gives a better insight
to what can be potentially pleasurable. Ask your
partner, or your friends, and share your stories with
them. The answers you get, even your own,
may surprise you!

How do you feel about sex talk on the phone?

_____

_____

_____

_____

_____

_____

_____

How do you feel about sending naughty texts?

_____

_____

_____

_____

_____

_____

_____

How do you feel about sending nude pics?

_____

_____

_____

_____

_____

_____

_____

WEEK 51

Listen to audio-only porn or a dirty podcast.

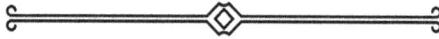

───────◇───────

By taking away the visuals you get to imagine whatever you want while listening to the stories. Let your mind go, get creative and imagine visuals that really excite you.

Date_____

What did you listen to?

_____
_____
_____
_____
_____
_____
_____

How did it make you feel?

_____
_____
_____
_____
_____
_____

Did you get busy while listening to it?

_____
_____
_____
_____
_____
_____
_____

WEEK 52

Create a Sex Jar!
Be sure to choose a jar that looks sexy or stylish,
something that inspires excitement, rather than
some old mayonnaise bottle.

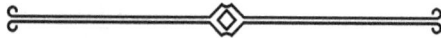

◇

Think about all the new toys, accessories and
experiences you've enjoyed this year. On small slips
of paper, write your favorite new erotic adventures,
plus any new ones you want to try, and add them
to the jar. Then pick a new slip of paper every week.
Definitely save your favorites to put back into
the jar later!

Date_____

What were some of your favorite ideas you wrote down?

_____
_____
_____
_____
_____
_____
_____

What does the jar look like and where do you keep it?

_____
_____
_____
_____
_____
_____

Which ideas do you already know you'll come back to again and again?

_____
_____
_____
_____
_____
_____

FUTURE FUN IDEAS:

Thank you for choosing The 52-Week Journal series for your journaling experience.

And congratulations to you for completing the first steps towards the more sexually creative and empowered life you deserve!

If you enjoyed this journal experience, please check out the other versions we have at www.52weekjournal.com

52·WEEK
JOURNAL